Tara Binns
Clued-up Detective

Written by Lisa Rajan
Illustrated by Alessia Trunfio

Collins

Chapter 1

Tara Binns knelt in front of the costume box in the attic at the top of her house. She had visited the box many times before. Each time she opened it, it gave her a different outfit for a different job: astronaut, engineer, diver, vet. But it did more than that. It gave her a taste of what it would be like to do that job, the challenges and the fun of solving problems.

The jobs were always ones she had never thought of before, opening her eyes to all kinds of possibilities ahead of her. Tara had never thought of herself as especially brave or adventurous, but her visits to the costume box made her start to see herself differently.

Tara took a deep breath and lifted the lid. She felt
a tingling in her hand that flowed up her arm. It spread
around her whole body and, within moments, she felt herself
spinning away from the dusty attic. She tumbled through
space and time as she began a new adventure as … what?

Tara closed her eyes tightly and wondered …

What will I be today?

Chapter 2

When Tara opened her eyes, she was outside on a quiet street lined with houses. She was wearing a police uniform.

"Hi!" said a girl dressed in the same way as Tara. "I'm Ayesha – I'm a police detective. This is Ortez – he's a crime scene examiner. We're investigating the disappearance of a boy who lives down this street."

"What's a crime scene examiner?" asked Tara.

"We collect evidence – fingerprints, footprints, blood, or DNA. Or things like dirt, liquids, powder, crumbs, or stains …" said Ortez, "… something dropped or thrown away. Or something usual in an unusual place. Anything that might be a clue to what has been going on."

"Clues help to tell a story," Ayesha added. "We see if they match what witnesses or suspects tell us."

"What's happened to the boy?" asked Tara.

"We don't know yet," replied Ayesha seriously, showing Tara a photo.

"This is Dylan. His sister Fran has just reported him missing. He usually walks back from football training with a friend, Sunita, but he never arrived home. We're about to ask Sunita what she knows."

Ayesha stepped up on to the doorstep and rang the bell.

A girl answered the door.

"Good afternoon," said Ayesha. "Sunita? We've come about your friend, Dylan. He hasn't arrived home today and his sister is very worried. We understand you walked back from football practice with him an hour ago?"

Sunita looked shocked. "Yes, I did. The football pitches are at the top of our road. We walk back together as far as my house and then Dylan goes on to his house a few doors down the road. Is he OK?" She sounded upset.

"We don't know," said Ayesha, quietly. "Did he say he was going anywhere else?"

"No … but he sometimes buys sweets or a magazine," replied Sunita.

"Where?" asked Tara.

"At the convenience shop past his house. It's over there … past the car repair yard and the DIY shop." Sunita pointed.

"Was he acting strangely? Or differently in any way?"

"No … but – come to think of it, he was muttering about something weird going on earlier."

"When?" asked Ayesha.

"Before football. We met up outside the car repair yard. He'd just bought a drink in the convenience store. But I didn't think anything of it. I've never seen anything odd in that shop and Dylan's got quite an imagination!"

"We'll go and take a look anyway," said Ortez, and he smiled. "Thank you."

"I hope he turns up soon," said Sunita.

Ayesha led them across the road towards the shop. They walked past the car repair yard. "Sorry!" she said, nearly bumping into someone who was hopping towards a rubbish bin.

"No problem!" he called, propping his foot up on the bin and picking chewing gum off the paint-spattered sole of his shoe.

"Do you work here?" asked Ayesha, showing him her police identification.

"Yes, I'm the mechanic. *Grrr* … this is disgusting!" he growled, a web of chewing gum between his fingers.

"Have you seen this boy today?" asked Ayesha, showing him a photo of Dylan.

The mechanic wobbled as he tried to focus on
the picture.

"Yes, I think so …" he said, "… in one of
the shops earlier. I've seen him around a lot. *Arghh!*
What a mess! Why do people drop gum? I'll have to go and
wash this off."

"Thank you," said Ayesha.

"No problem," smiled the mechanic cheerfully, rolling
up his sleeves. "I hope you find him soon!"

Chapter 3

Tara followed Ayesha and Ortez towards the DIY shop. They both stopped suddenly in the open doorway.

"Oh!" said Ortez in surprise.

Tara peered over his shoulder. What chaos! Someone had dropped a tin of yellow paint in the middle of the floor. It had leaked everywhere. It looked as if someone had slipped over in the mess and made it even worse. The shop owner was on his hands and knees with a cloth, trying to wipe it up.

"Don't come in!" he shouted crossly over his shoulder.

"What happened?" asked Tara.

"I tripped over and dropped it, didn't I?" he replied angrily. "Not that it's any of your business!" He dragged the cloth through the spreading puddle.

"We're the police," said Ayesha, showing her identification badge. "A local boy is missing."

Tara stepped into the shop and almost fell over the shop owner's shoes. She noticed they had no laces in them. *That's probably why he tripped,* she thought.

"Let me help you," Tara said, grabbing a dustpan and brush from the counter.

"No, no … don't. You'll just make it worse," the owner snapped.

You're the one making it worse by spreading it around with that cloth, thought Tara. *You need to scoop it up.*

Ayesha held out the photo of Dylan.

"Did this boy come into your shop earlier?" she asked.

"No," said the owner, not even looking at the photo.

Tara couldn't help herself. She got down on her hands and knees and started brushing the gooey mess into a dustpan. It worked well. She tipped a full dustpan into the bucket.

"Please look at the photo," said Ayesha firmly, showing it to him again.

"I've never seen him before," the owner grunted.

"He lives opposite," said Ortez. "You must have seen him!"

"Well I haven't. And like I said, I can clean up by myself," the owner growled at Tara. "Can you go now? It's closing time and you're in the way. Try next door."

How rude! thought Tara. *And how odd. Why does he want to get rid of us? Did he recognise Dylan? And did he really trip over or was there some sort of struggle? With Dylan, maybe?*

Chapter 4

As Tara opened the convenience shop door, she thought she saw the shop assistant hastily shove something under the counter out of sight.

"Can I … help … you?" the girl yawned.

"Yes," said Ayesha, showing her identification. "Police. We're looking for a boy who might be missing. We think he came in here, about an hour ago." She showed Dylan's photo.

"He was here this morning, but not this afternoon," the girl said grumpily.

"Are you sure?" asked Ayesha.

"Yes. No one has been in all afternoon. Maybe because of the rain."

Tara looked down. There were muddy footprints all over the floor, going between the door, the shelves and the counter.

"Who made these, then?" asked Tara, pointing at the footprints.

The girl shrugged. "They must be from this morning."

"It didn't start raining till 2 o'clock this afternoon," said Ayesha.

Ortez looked closely at the floor. "Look! There are two different sets of footprints. These are smaller than the others," he said, pointing.

Ortez pulled up the hood of his forensic suit and handed Tara a pair of plastic overshoes. "Put these on, in case some of these footprints belong to Dylan. We don't want to contaminate the scene with any of our own."

"I don't know … all I can tell you is I didn't see any customers this afternoon," said the shop assistant, shrugging.

Ortez put a ruler alongside one of the footprints and took a photo. Then he took a sample of the dirt in the footprint with a clean swab stick.

He returned the swab stick to its plastic tube, screwed the lid on and put it in an evidence bag. He labelled the bag with a pen.

"Did you leave the shop?" asked Ayesha.

The shop assistant shook her head. "Of course not – I'd get sacked," she said nervously.

Tara stayed by the counter. Her gaze fell on a neat stack of coins by the chewing gum stand. *Why are those there?* she wondered. She stepped over a basket full of shopping to take a closer look. She put on gloves and took an evidence bag from Ortez's case. She carefully lifted the coins and popped them inside.

"Look!" said Ayesha, suddenly. "By the magazine rack!"

Tara followed Ayesha's pointing finger. A backpack! Could it belong to Dylan?

Ortez unzipped the backpack and pulled out a notebook with Dylan's name written on it, a magazine and some muddy football boots.

"It looks as if he was here," said Ortez.

Why did the shop assistant lie? wondered Tara.

Chapter 5

Ayesha, Ortez and Tara took the backpack, the swab sticks and the coins back to the lab. The forensic scientists there analysed the mud on the swab sticks and checked the coins and notebook for fingerprints. They measured the length of the football boots to check Dylan's shoe size.

Tara watched one of the scientists swab the bottom of Dylan's backpack.

"He may have put it down somewhere else that could give us a clue to his movements this afternoon, after he left Sunita," Ortez explained.

Tara noticed a small bright smudge on one corner.

"Yellow paint!" she shouted. "It's exactly the same colour as the spill in the DIY shop. Dylan must have been in there, after all."

Her eyes widened as she put two and two together.

"The owner must have grabbed him … maybe Dylan struggled … knocking the paint tin off the shelf. Maybe he slipped in the spill … Maybe the owner tied him up with his shoelaces, so he couldn't get away. He might still be there, in a back room!" Tara's head was in an excited spin.

"But we found Dylan's backpack in the convenience shop," Ayesha pointed out. "How did it get there?"

"If the DIY shop owner had taken the backpack next door, he'd have left a trail of yellow sock prints between the two shops," Ayesha went on, "and we didn't see any."

Tara felt embarrassed. "But the two shades of yellow are the same?" she ventured shyly.

"Just because they *look* the same doesn't mean they *are* the same. Forensic science is all about evidence and proof. We would need to test both of them to prove that they are identical," Ortez explained gently.

Tara bit her lip. She felt stupid jumping to conclusions.

"But we *can't* test both," said Ayesha, looking accusingly at Ortez. "You didn't take a sample of the DIY shop paint spill!"

"It wasn't a crime scene!" Ortez said hotly. "And you didn't think of it, either."

"It's too late to go back now – the owner will have washed the floor," said Ayesha, frowning angrily.

"Hang on," said Tara slowly. "I might have taken a sample … without realising it …"

"What do you mean?" Ayesha spun round.

"I dipped my sleeve in the paint when I was cleaning up!" Tara lifted her arm to show her.

"Let's test it," grinned Ortez, and he pulled out a swab stick tube.

Chapter 6

Jamila from the laboratory gave them the results of their forensic tests.

"The smaller footprints are the same shoe size as Dylan's football boots ..." she confirmed, "... and they did have traces of yellow paint on them. So did some of the bigger footprints and the backpack – the same paint. But that paint *didn't* come from the DIY shop. It didn't match the paint from your sleeve. It was totally different. The backpack paint was waterproof, the sleeve one wasn't. We'll test it further and find out what type of paint it actually is."

"Any fingerprints on the coins?" asked Tara.

"Yes, and they match the only fingerprints on Dylan's notebook. That proves he was definitely in the shop," said Jamila.

"He probably left the coins on the counter to pay for something," suggested Tara. "I wonder what it was?"

"So why did the shop assistant say he hadn't been there? Very suspicious," said Ayesha.

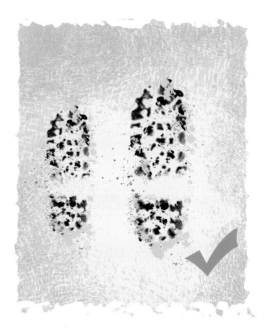

Tara asked to look at Dylan's notebook. *Maybe this will give us a clue to where he is?* she thought.

Inside, he had written a list. Each row of the list had four things in it: a date, a time, a colour … and then a mixture of numbers and capital letters. He had drawn lines linking the different rows together, so that each was paired with another.

What can it mean? wondered Tara.

The earliest date was several weeks ago, and the latest was yesterday. The times were all in the evening.
The colours were all different.

She showed the list to Ortez and Ayesha. Ortez was very excited by this new lead.

"That's great, Tara!" he said. "This list could be the key to solving the mystery."

"We should go and talk to Dylan's sister Fran," said Tara. "We can ask her about this notebook."

Chapter 7

"He always keeps that notebook with him," said Fran. "Why would he leave it in a shop? Something bad must have happened!"

"Did he have other friends living on the street? Or close by?" asked Ayesha.

"No … and he wouldn't have gone anywhere else without telling me," said Fran, helplessly.

She took them up to Dylan's bedroom to check for more clues. Tara scanned the room. The walls were covered in pictures of supercars, very flash and expensive looking. *Dylan must be keen on cars as well as football,* she thought.

Tara looked at the pictures more closely. She noticed three things.

Firstly, they were printed-out photos, not posters. Secondly, the background was the same in all of them – paint-spattered tarmac. And thirdly, the registration numbers of the cars in the photos seemed to match the combinations of numbers and letters in the list in Dylan's notebook. She pulled on gloves and grabbed the notebook from Ayesha to double-check.

Yes! Every registration number on the list was present on one of the supercars in the photos.

Then she spotted something about the registration numbers that Dylan had linked together in the notebook. In each case, the make and model of the supercars in the photos were the same!

But the colour was different.

What could it mean?

Tara dashed over to the window. Dylan's bedroom window looked out on to the forecourt of the car repair yard opposite. That meant he could see over the solid metal gates. Tara was staring at the exact same view that was the background for all the photos. The photos must have been taken from this window!

But why? Because he was interested in supercars … or for a different reason? *Why write down dates and times in his notebook?*

Tara went over everything again: the paint smudge on the bag, and on Dylan's footprints, the supercars that were so similar to each other …

Hmm, she pondered, trying to think logically.

She looked out at the car repair yard forecourt again. There were no supercars in it now – just an old saloon car. The mechanic walked over to it, got in and turned the engine and lights on.

Supercars … the same … but different colours …

Suddenly, it came to her! She spun around.

"Ayesha … Ortez," she said falteringly, "I … I think I know what Dylan's list is all about."

Chapter 8

Ortez, Ayesha and Fran stopped talking. All three of them stared at Tara.

"The paint sample …" she began, "… what if it was car body paint? It was waterproof, after all. What if the car repair yard opposite is respraying stolen supercars, putting new registration plates on them and selling them on?"

Ayesha considered.

"The pairs of photos weren't of two *different* cars …" continued Tara, "… they were of the same car – just sprayed a different colour. Dylan was the only person who could see what was going on! His window looks down on to the garage forecourt."

Ortez's jaw dropped. "I'll phone Jamila," he said, pulling out his phone. "I'll find out if she has analysed the paint sample from Dylan's backpack."

A few minutes later, he confirmed what Tara suspected. "Jamila says it *is* car paint, and it's a few days old. Looks like Dylan stumbled across a supercar theft racket."

"He always wanted to be a detective," cried Fran. "I told him to leave it to the police … but I bet he couldn't resist doing his own investigation when he saw what was going on over the road! But where is he?"

Tara went back to the window. There was a pair of binoculars and a chewing gum wrapper on the windowsill behind the curtain.

Chewing gum … she thought … and that reminds me of something … what is it? Tara racked her brain.

Yes! The chewing gum next to the till in the convenience shop. Now that she thought about it, the coins in the pile on the shop counter could have been left by Dylan to pay for a packet of chewing gum. Sunita had said he often went to the shop to buy sweets and magazines … perhaps he had gone in to get some chewing gum. But why had he left the money on the counter instead of giving it to the shop assistant?

Hmm ... I don't know ... thought Tara ... *and that links Dylan to the convenience shop, not the car repair yard.*

Tara shook her head and started again.

Paint ... footprints ... shoes ... shops ... It was no good, she kept coming back to chewing gum. *Why?* Something was niggling at her.

Chewing gum ...

Unless ... Of course! It dawned on her. Tara's eyes widened with excitement.

"I think I know where Dylan is!" she shouted.

Chapter 9

"Follow me!" ordered Tara, charging out of Dylan's bedroom and down the stairs. If she was right, Dylan could be in danger.

"Where are you going?" cried Ayesha.

"Remember when we first saw the mechanic?" panted Tara, opening the front door. "He was picking chewing gum off the bottom of his shoe. What if the gum belonged to Dylan? What if Dylan went to the shop, bought some chewing gum, put his backpack down to look at the magazines and saw the gate of the car repair yard open? He'd had a hunch about the supercars being resprayed and this was his chance to check it out. So he went in to investigate!"

"It's possible," said Ortez, following Tara and Ayesha across the road. "But where is he?"

"What if he found some evidence to back up his theory? Yellow car paint … or fake registration plates? But then the mechanic caught him snooping and knew the game would be up if Dylan went to the police? Maybe they struggled and Dylan's gum fell out of his mouth. Maybe –"

They arrived outside the car repair yard.

"Open up!" shouted Ayesha, banging on the fence.

"Oh! It's you again," said the mechanic, reluctantly opening the gate.

"Yes, and we want to look around," said Ayesha firmly, walking into the yard.

"*Er … of course …*" he replied hesitantly. "*Umm … why?*"

"The missing boy – Dylan – is he here?" demanded Ortez, following Ayesha in.

"No. I told you that earlier," said the mechanic, his eyes darting about shiftily.

Tara's eyes followed his around the yard. The paint-spattered respraying booth was empty. There were no cupboards, no cabinets, no back room, no tyre stacks – nowhere to hide a boy. There was also no spray gun and no registration plates in sight.

Maybe Dylan *hadn't* found anything and he had left again. Or maybe he'd never even been here.

I was wrong and now we've wasted precious time, Tara thought to herself crossly.

"See? No one's here but me," smirked the mechanic. "Now if you wouldn't mind leaving … I'm about to lock up and go home."

He began walking towards the open car door. The engine was still running.

As Tara walked past the back of the car, she noticed the light on one side was no longer working.

That's strange! It was on when I saw the car from Dylan's bedroom a minute ago … Why is it off now?

Tara stopped in her tracks and stared at the broken light. It came to her in a flash.

There was nowhere to hide … except …

"The boot of the car!" she shouted, rushing to open it. The mechanic lurched forward to stop her. Ayesha sprang into action and wrestled him to the ground. Tara felt for the button and opened the boot. She looked in.

Her eyes met those of a startled, scared boy, curled up next to a holdall.

"Yes! He's here!" she shouted triumphantly. She grinned down at him.

The mechanic looked shocked.

"What's he doing in there?" he spluttered. "I was about to drive home!"

Ortez looked accusingly at the mechanic. "Did you put Dylan in the boot because he'd rumbled you?" he asked coldly.

"No!" said the mechanic. "I had no idea he was there!" He looked so amazed that Tara couldn't help believing him.

Chapter 10

Tara helped Dylan climb out. He looked wobbly and scared.

"I'm so sorry," he said sheepishly. "I thought something dodgy was going on in here, but I could never get through the gate. Today it was open and so I took the chance and slipped in to investigate. I didn't mean any harm. Please don't arrest me!"

"We're not going to arrest you!" Tara reassured Dylan. "We've been looking for you! Fran reported you missing. What happened?"

Dylan hesitated. "I've … I've been watching this place from my window. Cars were going in one colour and coming out another colour. I'm a bit of a detective and thought something strange was going on. I looked through the crack in the fence everyday but I couldn't see what was happening.

"Then I got my chance. I was in the shop when the mechanic came in. He picked up a basket. I could see that he had left the yard gate open …

"So, I thought I had just enough time to poke around in the yard. But I didn't find anything and then I heard footsteps. He was coming back! I guess he couldn't find the shop assistant either. I had to hide … the boot of this car was open … it was a split-second decision …

"I was going to wait till he'd gone and then try to get out. But he turned the engine on! I'm such a fool. I should have left the detective work to the professionals," Dylan finished.

"Why didn't you shout out when you realised you were trapped?" asked Tara. "Or when we arrived?"

"I didn't know you were the police," said Dylan, apologetically. "I thought you were friends of his. I couldn't hear very well from inside the boot."

Dylan stretched awkwardly. *He must have been uncomfortable as well as scared,* thought Tara. There was a big holdall in the boot and Dylan must have been squashed into a tiny space.

The holdall …

She lifted it awkwardly out of the boot. It was heavy. The mechanic froze. Tara dropped it on the ground and opened the zip. Her jaw dropped when she saw what was inside.

"False registration plates! Bundles of cash!" she cried. "And a spray gun … with yellow paint on the nozzle! The boot really was the only hiding place here!"

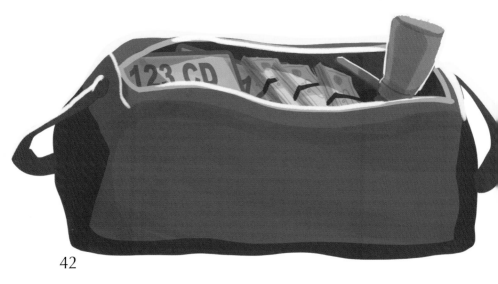

"That car belongs to a customer," blustered
the mechanic. "I've never seen that stuff before in my life!"

"Then why didn't you want Tara to open the boot?"
asked Ortez. "You *knew* the holdall was in there and that
your fingerprints would be all over everything."

"No, they won't!" The mechanic smirked and raised
his hands. He was wearing protective gloves.

Ayesha stamped her foot in frustration. He was right.
If they couldn't prove his fingerprints were on the holdall,
the mechanic would get away with it.

How can we prove anything without proper evidence?
thought Tara. *There must be a way …*

Tara stared at his gloved hands …

Wait a minute … she thought … *His sleeves!*

Tara remembered that they were rolled up earlier when he went to wash the chewing gum off his hands. She looked at her own sleeve, which still had paint from the DIY shop on it.

Maybe the mechanic was wearing the same overalls when he resprayed the last supercar … Maybe his sleeves were down … Maybe he got yellow paint on them – that would link him to the spray gun, wouldn't it?

"Roll down your sleeves," she ordered.

He glared at her.

"Do it," said Ayesha. "*Now!*"

The mechanic reluctantly rolled them down. There were tiny specks of yellow at the end of his sleeves.

Tara pointed triumphantly. "Car paint – like on the footprints!"

"*Grrr* … that stupid nozzle!" the mechanic growled. "I was going to get it fixed. It kept getting clogged up … dripping paint everywhere –"

"Is that how you got it on the soles of your shoes …
and on the ground outside the gate?" Tara asked, realising
that Dylan probably put his backpack down on a yellow
footprint a few days ago, when he'd been trying to look
through the fence.

Chapter 11

"You need to come with us to the police station," Ayesha told the mechanic. "You've got a lot of questions to answer."

He scowled. He knew it was going to be hard to talk his way out of trouble.

"How did you know where I was, Tara?" asked Dylan.

"Chewing gum …" answered Tara. "You dropped some on the ground. Am I right? It stuck to the mechanic's shoe. We saw him picking it off."

Dylan nodded. "It fell out of my mouth when I was looking for a place to hide. But how did you know I was in the boot?"

"The car's back lights," said Tara. "They were both on when I saw them from your bedroom window, but only one was working when we got down here. Did you kick it from the inside to try and get out of the boot?"

He nodded again, astonished.

"You gave us lots of clues that led us right to you – your backpack, your notebook, your photos – so your detective skills helped us crack the case! But you should have called the police straightaway instead of taking the risks you did," said Tara. "You could have been in serious danger."

"I know." Dylan bit his lip. "I'm sorry. I won't be so stupid again."

Tara led everyone out of the car repair yard.

"Can we pop into the shop on the way home?" asked Dylan. "I want to get some chewing gum. In case I need to leave a trail on my next case!"

Tara laughed. "Yes, we can. Do you know if they sell radios? And shoelaces?"

"Why?" asked Fran.

"The radio is for the shop assistant …" Tara explained, smiling, "… to help keep her awake. She works such long hours that she takes naps behind the counter when the shop is empty. That's why she was so tired and grumpy. And that's why Dylan had to leave the money for his chewing gum on the counter … and why she didn't realise that she'd even had customers."

"That's a clever deduction," said Ayesha.

"Actually, I saw her stuffing a pillow under the counter when we first walked in!" laughed Tara.

"And the shoelaces?" asked Ortez.

"Those are for the DIY shop owner …" said Tara, "… so he can keep his shoes on properly and won't have any more unfortunate trip-ups!"

"You can tell us who else was in the supercar theft racket back at the police station," Ayesha told the mechanic.

"You can't prove anything," muttered the mechanic.

"Yes, we can," said Ortez. "We'll check the call history on your phone. There will be evidence to convict you all."

"Thanks to you, Tara," smiled Ayesha. "You spotted clues that we didn't even realise *were* clues and put the whole thing together!"

She raised her hand for a high-five.

As Tara happily clapped her hand against Ayesha's, she felt a tingling in her fingertips. It spread through her hand and down her arm. She felt it swirl around her whole body and take her with it, around and around. She could no longer feel the pavement beneath her feet, but instead, felt herself tumbling and spinning, back through space and time … until …

A-BOOM!

Chapter 12

When the spinning stopped, Tara found herself back in the attic. She took off her uniform and noticed that the yellow paint smudge on the sleeve had gone.

I guess the clues will be different next time, she thought, already hoping the box would give her this costume again sometime. *But the challenges will be the same … collecting evidence, getting it analysed, interpreting the results, thinking logically …*

There was so much more to being a detective than she had ever imagined.

She closed the lid of the box and smiled.

Maybe I'll be a detective when I grow up ... I'm good at spotting things other people don't and I'm learning not to jump to conclusions. When the evidence raises difficult questions, I don't give up until I work out the answers. Who'd have thought it would be my deductions that cracked the case? But I've always liked questioning things I don't understand ... so maybe the clues to my detecting ability were there all along!

Which clues led Tara to Dylan?

Ideas for reading

Written by Clare Dowdall, PhD
Lecturer and Primary Literacy Consultant

Reading objectives:
- draw inferences and justify these with evidence
- predict what might happen from details stated and implied
- summarise the main ideas drawn from more than one paragraph, identifying key details that support the main ideas
- discuss and evaluate how authors use language, including figurative language, considering the impact on the reader

Spoken language objectives:
- use relevant strategies to build their vocabulary
- participate in discussions, presentations, performances, role play, improvisations and debates

Curriculum links: Science: Properties and materials

Interest words: contaminate, evidence, deduction, forensic scientists, convict, racket

Resources: paper, pencils and water-based paints; whiteboards and pens; notebooks

Build a context for reading

- Look at the cover and read the title *Clued-up Detective*. Ask children to explain what the phrase *Clued-up* means.
- Focus on the word *Detective*. Find the root word *detect* inside it. Check children know what it means and can use the word in a sentence.
- Read the blurb together. Discuss what sort of information detectives and forensic scientists can gather from fingerprints, footprints and paint smudges. Introduce some of the interest words to use in this discussion.
- Ask children to share what they know about the work of a detective. Make a list of some of the challenges and rewards of this job.

Understand and apply reading strategies

- Ask for a volunteer to read pp2–3. Focus on the author's use of language: *opening her eyes to all kinds of possibilities ahead of her*. Pause to discuss how the language works literally (implying a surprised expression) and metaphorically (showing new things) to convey meaning.
- Help children to relate to the character of Tara in chapter one by challenging them to think of a time when they have seen themselves differently, or to think of a time when someone else has seen them from a different perspective. Ask for examples.